WASHINGTON
WIZARDS

by Ray Frager

Published by ABDO Publishing Company, 8000 West 78th Street, Edina, Minnesota 55439. Copyright © 2012 by Abdo Consulting Group, Inc. International copyrights reserved in all countries. No part of this book may be reproduced in any form without written permission from the publisher. SportsZone™ is a trademark and logo of ABDO Publishing Company.

Printed in the United States of America,
North Mankato, Minnesota
062011
092011

 THIS BOOK CONTAINS AT LEAST 10% RECYCLED MATERIALS.

Editor: Matt Tustison
Copy Editor: Nicholas Cafarelli
Series design: Christa Schneider
Cover production: Kazuko Collins
Interior production: Carol Castro

Photo Credits: Phelan M. Ebenhack/AP Images, cover; Focus on Sport/Getty Images, 1; AP Images, 4, 10, 15, 16, 22, 42 (top), 43 (top); NBAE/Getty Images, 7, 9, 13, 27; William Smith/AP Images, 18, 42 (middle); Jim McKnight/AP Images, 21, 42 (bottom); Dave Tenenbaum/AP Images, 25; C.W. Agel/AP Images, 28; Roberto Borea/AP Images, 31; Getty Images, 33, 34; Beth A. Keiser/AP Images, 37, 43 (middle); Nick Wass/AP Images, 39, 41, 43 (bottom), 44; Pablo Martinez Monsivais/AP Images, 47

Library of Congress Cataloging-in-Publication Data
Frager, Ray.
  Washington Wizards / by Ray Frager.
    p. cm. -- (Inside the NBA)
  Includes index.
  ISBN 978-1-61783-178-2
  1. Washington Wizards (Basketball team)--History--Juvenile literature. I. Title.
  GV885.52.W37F73 2011
  796.323'6409753--dc22
                          2011014723

TABLE OF CONTENTS

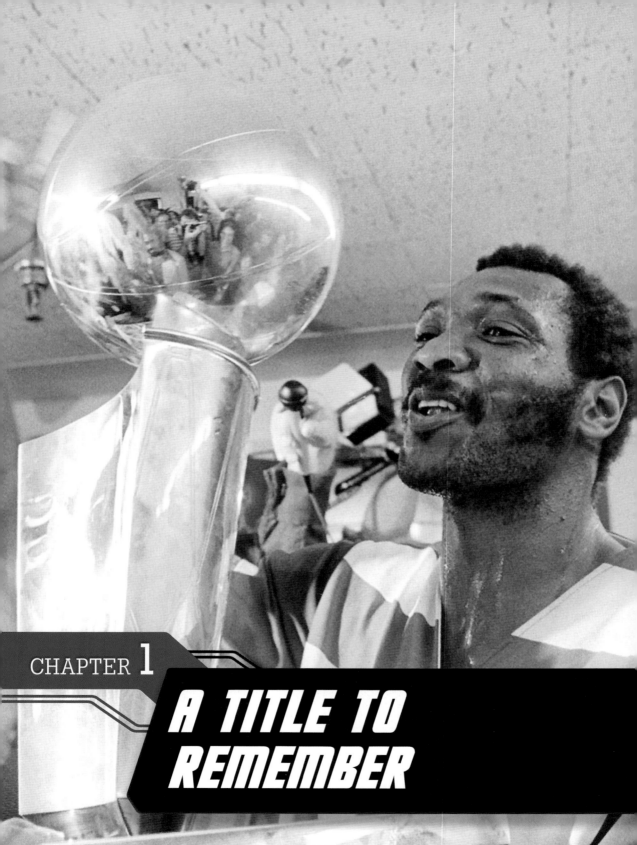

CHAPTER 1

A TITLE TO REMEMBER

The Washington Wizards franchise has been around since 1961. It has had four team nicknames and called three cities home. The club hit its height in 1978. The team, then known as the Washington Bullets, won the National Basketball Association (NBA) title that year.

Though the Bullets had some talented players, they did not look like champions during the 1977–78 regular season. They posted a winning record. But it was only 44–38. And they were not a good team on the road, going 15–26. They also lost one of their most reliable players, guard Phil Chenier, to an injury about halfway through the season.

The Bullets' biggest star was Elvin Hayes, a 6-foot-9 forward/center. During their championship season, Hayes averaged 19.7 points and 13.3 rebounds per game.

Washington Bullets star Elvin Hayes admires the championship trophy his team won by defeating the Seattle SuperSonics in the 1978 NBA Finals. Nineteen years later, the Bullets changed their name to the Wizards.

He shared the scoring load with Bob Dandridge. Dandridge was a forward who had been signed as a free agent from the Milwaukee Bucks. He scored 19.3 points per game that first season with Washington.

The Bullets received balanced scoring from several other players. Mitch Kupchak averaged 15.9 points per game, Kevin Grevey 15.5, and Tom Henderson 11.4. Wes Unseld did not score much, averaging 7.6 points. But he was an intimidating force around the basket. At 6 feet 7, he was not the tallest center or forward. But Unseld was a solid 245 pounds. He collected 11.9 rebounds per game.

"We had such diverse talent on that team," Hayes said. "From the bench to the starters, we had great balance."

In the playoffs, the Bullets got past the Atlanta Hawks and the San Antonio Spurs before meeting the Philadelphia 76ers in the Eastern Conference finals. The 76ers featured superstar forwards Julius Erving and George McGinnis and high-scoring guard Doug Collins. Nevertheless, the Bullets eliminated the 76ers in six games. Washington won the deciding contest 101–99 at home.

That put the Bullets in the NBA Finals against the Seattle SuperSonics. The Sonics had a dynamic backcourt in Gus Williams and Dennis Johnson. Long-range shooter Freddie "Downtown" Brown was a standout reserve. In the middle, the Sonics featured 7-foot-1 shot-blocker Marvin "The Human Eraser" Webster.

In Game 1, the Bullets wasted a 19-point lead and lost in Seattle. The teams split the next two contests at Washington's Capital Centre. Game 4 was held in Seattle's Kingdome.

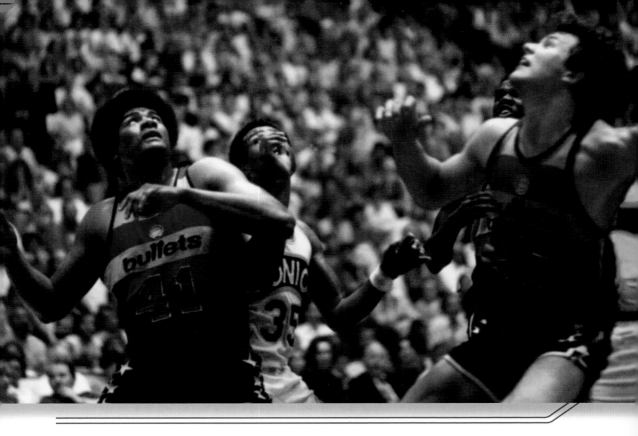

Washington's Wes Unseld, *left*, and Mitch Kupchak, *right*, battle for rebound positioning in Game 1 of the 1978 NBA Finals.

It was the home of football's Seahawks and baseball's Mariners. The game was moved to the Kingdome because the Sonics' usual home arena, the Seattle Coliseum, was being used for a mobile-home show. Attendance for Game 4 set a Finals record of 39,457. The back-and-forth nature of the series continued with a Bullets victory in overtime, though. Washington had trailed by double digits late in the third quarter. The Sonics then prevailed in Game 5 back at the Coliseum. The Bullets were one game away from losing the Finals.

Washington coach Dick Motta had been repeating a phrase to reporters about the

"THE BIG E"

Elvin Hayes was known as "The Big E," and he was a big-time player in the NBA.

Hayes played 16 seasons in the league from 1968 to 1984. He ranked as the seventh all-time scorer in league history through the 2009–10 season with 27,313 points. His 16,279 career rebounds were the fourth most ever. He was named to the Basketball Hall of Fame in 1990.

Hayes's favorite move on offense was a turnaround jump shot. He would use it to get shots off against anyone, even taller players he faced either at forward or center.

In addition to his scoring, rebounding, and shot-blocking, Hayes was known for not getting along with coaches. He had arguments with several of them. "My father always taught me to be strong and to have dignity, to not have to bow down or have anyone run over you," Hayes said.

Bullets' chances since earlier in the playoffs: "The opera isn't over 'til the fat lady sings." This meant that the Bullets would not give up until they were officially eliminated. And they would show that same kind of fight in the Finals.

Washington rolled to an easy 117–82 victory in Game 6 at the Capital Centre. The Bullets won even though starting guard Grevey was hurt badly enough that Dandridge moved to the unfamiliar position. Substitute Greg Ballard started for Dandridge at forward. Ballard filled in well. He scored 12 points and grabbed 12 rebounds.

The decisive Game 7 in Seattle was much closer, however. The Sonics made a late run to cut the Bullets' lead to two points with little time left. But Unseld, though he had

Teammates Bob Dandridge, *left*, and Elvin Hayes celebrate after the Bullets captured the 1978 NBA title with a Game 7 win over the Sonics.

made only about half his foul shots in the playoffs, hit two free throws to help put the game away. Washington won 105–99 and captured the team's first NBA title. Through the 2010–11 season, it remained the franchise's only league crown.

The Bullets had the worst regular-season record of any team that went on to win an NBA championship. But they were champions nevertheless.

"Just Tremendous"

"*I remember flying out to Seattle thinking about all the things that I had gone through all the years that I had played in the NBA. All of that was coming down to one game, a championship game, and after that game, I remember feeling a joy over the next 48 hours, just a spring of joy, a feeling of great accomplishment. Out of my 16 years of playing, I had waited for that moment, and that moment came, and it was just tremendous.*"
—*Bullets star big man Elvin Hayes, on Game 7 of the 1978 NBA Finals*

CHAPTER 2

WIZARDS' ROOTS

The Washington Wizards' beginnings go back to Chicago in 1961. The team that eventually became the Wizards started out as an NBA expansion club, the Chicago Packers.

The Packers were not exactly a big success. They finished 18–62 in their first season. Their average attendance of about 2,500 ranked last in the league. The roster was made up of almost all young, inexperienced players. Of the 17 who played for the Packers in the 1961–62 season, only three had at least five years of NBA experience. Six players were rookies.

One of those rookies, though, could really play. Walt Bellamy was a 6-foot-11-inch center from Indiana University. He averaged 31.6 points and 19 rebounds per game. He was named the league's Rookie of the Year.

Chicago Packers rookie center Walt Bellamy, *left,* poses with Philadelphia Warriors star Wilt Chamberlain in March 1962. The 1961–62 season was the first for the Packers, the ancestors of today's Washington Wizards.

THE FIRST BULLETS

Before the Chicago Zephyrs moved to Baltimore and became the Bullets in 1963, there was an earlier pro basketball team called the Baltimore Bullets. They played from 1947 to 1954.

Their first two seasons were played in the BAA, which merged with the National Basketball League (NBL) to create the NBA in 1949. The Bullets won the BAA title in 1948. Buddy Jeannette, who also played guard, was their coach. The Bullets played until November 1954, when the team, then in the NBA, folded.

The story goes that the original Bullets chose their name because a factory that made ammunition was near where they played. But that might not be true. A newspaper story from the founding of the team said, "The club will be known as the Bullets, which is hoped to be significant of their explosive talents and speed in humbling the opposition."

The next season, the team changed its name to the Zephyrs. Zephyr is a word meaning the west wind. It sounds swifter than a Packer. But the name change did not help any. The team went 25–55 and finished in last place in the Western Division again. Bellamy had another fine season, though. In addition, forward Terry Dischinger, who averaged 25.5 points, gave the team its second consecutive Rookie of the Year.

After its second season in Chicago, the team moved to Baltimore. The club's nickname was changed to the Bullets. There was a previous team in Baltimore called the Bullets. That team even won a title in the Basketball Association of America (BAA) in 1948. Those Bullets later played in the NBA. But they went out of business in 1954.

The 1948 BAA champion Baltimore Bullets pose for a team photo. Player-coach Buddy Jeannette is at the far right.

In 1963, the new Bullets drafted forward Gus Johnson from the University of Idaho. He would go on to become one of the team's top players. With Bellamy, Dischinger, and now Johnson playing in the front-court, the team had more talent. The three star players combined to average about 65 points. Bellamy and Johnson teamed up to average 30 rebounds a contest. Still, the Bullets' results were not a whole lot better than the Zephyrs'. Baltimore's record in its first season, 1963–64, was 31–49. The team placed fourth out of five teams in the Western Division.

Before the 1964–65 season, the Bullets swung an eight-player trade. Dischinger, the team's second-leading scorer,

A Sweet Player

Before their first season in Baltimore, the Bullets drafted Gus "Honeycomb" Johnson. A powerfully built, 6-foot-6 forward, Johnson was among the first players to regularly go flying to the basket to score on eye-catching dunk shots. He could break backboards with his slams. "As power forwards go, he was a pioneer, a prototype," said forward Jack Marin, one of Johnson's teammates with the Bullets. "Gus was high entertainment, a showman, long before the game took that path." Johnson, who played nine seasons for the Bullets, was elected to the Basketball Hall of Fame in 2010.

was among those sent to the Detroit Pistons. The Bullets received five players, among them forward Bailey Howell and guard Don Ohl. With these additions, the Bullets had four players who averaged more than 18 points—Bellamy, Howell, Johnson, and Ohl. The team's record crept up to 37–43. The Bullets made the playoffs for the first time in the club's history. They got by the St. Louis Hawks in the first round before falling to the Los Angeles Lakers four games to two in the Western Division finals.

The Bullets made the playoffs again in 1965–66. But they still did not have a winning regular-season record (38–42). They lost in the first round to the Hawks this time. Early in the season, they traded their best player, Bellamy, to the New York Knicks. The scoring load was spread out more. Seven Bullets averaged double figures in points.

In 1966–67, the Bullets got out of the Western Division. Baltimore is in the eastern part of the United States. But the Bullets were in the Western Division because they previously played in Chicago. The Bullets' geography was straightened out when they were placed in

Bullets forward Gus Johnson flies toward the basket over the Knicks' Dick Barnett in February 1966.

the Eastern Division. But the team did worse. The Bullets' record dropped to 20–61. The team suffered a 13-game losing streak during the season. Baltimore went through three coaches during the 1966–67 season—Mike Farmer, Buddy Jeannette, and Gene Shue.

Tough Guy

"Gus was the toughest player I ever saw. He was a man's man, on and off the court. He was breaking backboards with one-handed dunks long before these guys today started doing it with two."
—Former Bullets star center Wes Unseld, on teammate Gus Johnson

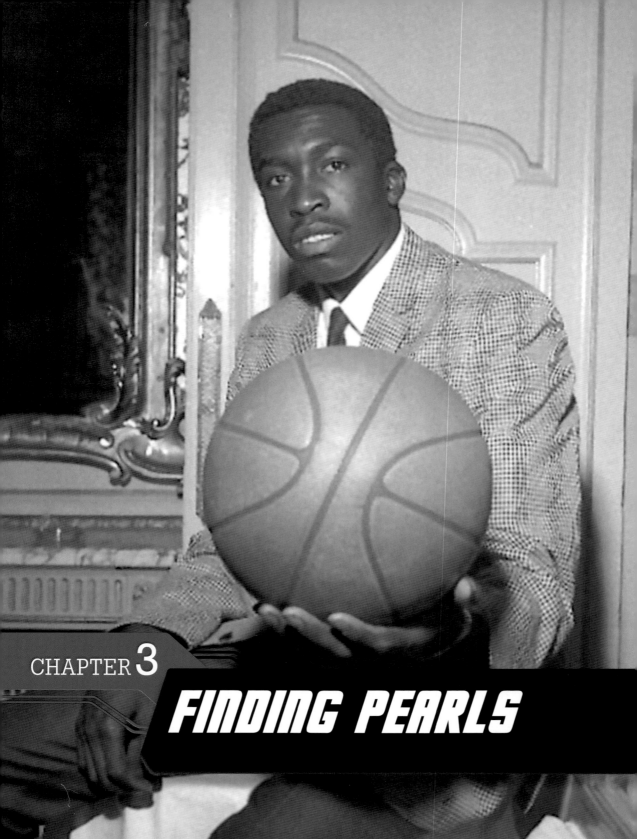

CHAPTER **3**

FINDING PEARLS

I

n the 1967 and 1968 NBA Drafts, the Bullets picked two players who would vault them to one of the top teams in the league.

First came Earl "The Pearl" Monroe. A guard from Winston-Salem State in North Carolina, Monroe brought playground creativity to the league. He would beat defenders with spinning moves and no-look passes. Then, in 1968, the Bullets selected Wes Unseld, a center from the University of Louisville. Unseld was not a big scorer. But he could dominate a game with his rebounding and defense. Unseld would spark his team's fast break. He fired

Unpredictable but Spectacular

"I don't know what I'm going to do with the ball, and if I don't know, I'm quite sure the guy guarding me doesn't know either."
—Former Bullets star guard Earl "The Pearl" Monroe, on his style of play

Earl "The Pearl" Monroe poses in May 1967. That month, the Bullets drafted the guard. He would become an instant star as a rookie.

Baltimore's Wes Unseld shoots over a fellow rookie, San Diego's Elvin Hayes, in the 1968–69 season. The two would later be Bullets teammates.

outlet passes to half-court right after he grabbed a rebound.

In Monroe's first season, he scored 24.3 points per game and was named NBA Rookie of the Year. The Bullets improved to 36–46. But they did not make the playoffs. Through seven seasons, the team still had not posted a winning season.

That changed in 1968–69. With Unseld in place, along with guards Monroe and Kevin Loughery and forwards Gus Johnson and Jack Marin, the Bullets went 57–25. They finished in first place in the Eastern Division. The return to the playoffs was short, however. The New York Knicks swept the Bullets in four games in the first round.

Unseld scored just 13.8 points per game. But he pulled down 18.2 rebounds a contest. He was selected both NBA Rookie of the Year and Most Valuable Player (MVP).

With the same lineup in place, the Bullets went 50–32 in 1969–70. They again met the Knicks in the first round of the playoffs. They again lost to them. The series went the full seven games this time, though.

The next season, the NBA rearranged its teams into new divisions. The Bullets won the Eastern Conference's Central Division with a 42–40 record. The Bullets got past the Knicks in the playoffs this time. Visiting Baltimore won Game 7 in the Eastern Conference finals 93–91.

The Bullets and the Knicks faced each other in the playoffs for six straight years. The series in 1971 was the only one the Bullets won. That victory put Baltimore into the NBA Finals for the first time. The Bullets faced the mighty Milwaukee Bucks. Milwaukee featured guard Oscar Robertson and center Kareem Abdul-Jabbar. The Bucks swept the Bullets in four games.

The Bullets' Loughery said, "You have to understand, Baltimore was always losing to New York—we couldn't beat the Knicks, the Colts couldn't defeat the Jets, the Orioles couldn't defeat the Mets. When we finally beat the defending champion Knicks, that was our championship."

Early in the 1971–72 season, the Bullets traded Monroe

EARL THE PEARL

Earl "The Pearl" Monroe's style of basketball was compared to jazz. Just as that music could surprise listeners by going off in a different direction, Monroe could pull moves on the court that his opponents found totally unexpected.

Monroe was neither very tall (6 feet 3 inches) nor very fast. He did not jump particularly high. But before anyone else in the NBA was doing it, Monroe would spin while he dribbled to get away from defenders. He would get them into the air with fake shots and go around for layups. He would look one way and drop a behind-the-back pass the other.

Monroe played for the Bullets from 1967 to 1971 before spending the final nine seasons of his career with the New York Knicks. He won an NBA title with the Knicks in 1973. He entered the Basketball Hall of Fame in 1990.

to the Knicks. Monroe wanted more money than the Bullets were willing to pay. So off he went to New York. Even without Monroe, the Bullets kept making the playoffs. In fact, the 1972–73 team, bolstered by the arrival of talented forward-center Elvin Hayes, went 52–30. Still, each season ended with a playoff loss to the Knicks. Then Baltimore lost the Bullets.

In April 1973, owner Abe Pollin moved the team to Landover, Maryland. Pollin had bought part of the team in 1964 and became sole owner in 1968. The Bullets' new home was about 40 miles (64 km) from Baltimore and close to Washington DC. The team was renamed the Capital Bullets. A year later, the club was renamed again, becoming the Washington Bullets. The team's home

Elvin Hayes guards the Buffalo Braves' Randy Smith in a 1975 playoff game. Hayes helped his team, which had changed names to the Washington Bullets, reach the NBA Finals that year, but the club lost.

arena in Landover was called the Capital Centre.

The Bullets were in the midst of making the playoffs for 12 straight seasons. They would reach the postseason each year from 1969 to 1980. After losing to New York again in the 1974 playoffs, Washington finished a franchise-best 60–22 in 1974–75. Hayes and guard Phil Chenier each averaged more than 20 points per game. The Bullets advanced to the NBA Finals for the second time but again were swept in four games. The Golden State Warriors, led by forward Rick Barry, beat the Bullets this time.

CHAPTER 4

TRYING TO REPEAT

After their 1978 NBA championship, the Bullets rolled through another strong season. They won the Atlantic Division in 1978–79 with a 54–28 record. The mark was the best in the NBA's regular season.

Putting the same lineup on the court as the previous season, the Bullets looked as if they could repeat as champions. They again featured balanced scoring. Elvin Hayes and Bob Dandridge each averaged about 20 points per game. Kevin Grevey and Mitch Kupchak were at about 15. Wes Unseld, Tom Henderson, Charles Johnson, and Larry Wright contributed about 10 apiece.

In the playoffs, the Bullets won seven-game series against the Atlanta Hawks and the San Antonio Spurs to return to the NBA Finals. They again faced

The Bullets' Wes Unseld (41) tries to block a shot by the Sonics' Paul Silas in the 1979 NBA Finals. Seattle won in five games, preventing Washington from a second title in a row.

the Seattle SuperSonics. At least one of the Sonics had fully expected it.

Before the postseason, Seattle guard Fred Brown said, "You know it all boils down to us against Washington one more time. . . . They're deeper, but we make up for that with our backcourt. I think it will be wild and picturesque all over again."

In Game 1 of the Finals, the host Bullets wasted an 18-point lead. With the score tied, Seattle's Dennis Johnson fouled Wright as time expired. Wright made the two free throws to give Washington a 99–97 victory. But the Bullets dropped the next four contests. The Sonics avenged the previous season's defeat by becoming NBA champions.

After losing in the Finals, the Bullets suffered a drop-off. Their record fell to 39–43 in each of the next two seasons.

They made the playoffs in 1979–80. But they did not do so in 1980–81. Age and injuries were catching up with some of the players.

This era of the Bullets ended for good after the 1980–81 season. The club's pillars in the frontcourt, Hayes and Unseld, left the team. Unseld retired after 13 seasons. Hayes was traded to the Houston Rockets.

The Bullets showed some improvement in 1981–82, however. Washington posted a 43–39 record. This earned Gene Shue the NBA Coach of the Year Award. The Bullets featured another rugged frontcourt with Greg Ballard, Jeff Ruland, and Rick Mahorn. Washington made it to the second round of the playoffs before losing to the Larry Bird-led Boston Celtics.

Washington missed the playoffs the next season before

The Bullets' Rick Mahorn, *left*, and Frank Johnson guard the Celtics' Robert Parish in a 1982 playoff game. Boston won the second-round series four games to one.

making the postseason the next five years in a row. However, each season ended with a first-round loss in the playoffs.

As happens in the NBA, players came and went from season to season. But no one was quite as unique a player as center Manute Bol.

The Bullets selected Bol in the second round of the 1985 NBA Draft from the University of Bridgeport in Connecticut. A native of the African country of Sudan, Bol stood 7 feet 7 inches. He was said to weigh about 225 pounds. Bol had stick-like arms and legs. His

BOL THE ACTIVIST

Manute Bol might have looked a bit comical on the basketball court with long, thin legs and skinny arms. But he was quite serious about trying to help people in his native country of Sudan.

When Bol died at age 47 in 2010, Ed Stefanski, the president of one of Bol's former teams, the Philadelphia 76ers, said Bol "was continually giving of himself through his generosity and humanitarian efforts in order to make the world around him a much better place, for which he will always be remembered."

Bol contributed time and money to organizations that worked to do things such as build schools in Sudan. "God guided me to America and gave me a good job," Bol once said. "But he also gave me a heart, so I would look back."

basketball skills were mostly limited to blocking shots. He averaged five blocks per game as a rookie, leading the NBA. Bol played three seasons for the Bullets and a total of 624 games for four NBA teams. For his career, he ended up with more blocks (2,086) than points (1,599).

In 1987, the Bullets drafted a player on the other end of the scale from Bol. Muggsy Bogues, a Baltimore native and former standout at Wake Forest University in North Carolina, was a 5-foot-3 guard. Washington selected him in the first round. He was the shortest player in league history. Bogues was incredibly quick, though. As a rookie, he led the Bullets in assists at 5.1 per game.

The Bullets included the unique Bol-Bogues combination and proven scorers

The Bullets' Manute Bol, 7 feet 7 inches, and Muggsy Bogues, 5 feet 3 inches, pose in 1987. Through the 2010–11 season, Bol and Bogues were the tallest and shortest players in NBA history.

in guard Jeff Malone and forwards Bernard King and Moses Malone. But they still were just in the middle of the NBA's teams. Early in the 1987–88 season, coach Kevin Loughery was fired. Unseld took over. The team played better for Unseld. But the result was a 38–44 record and a customary first-round defeat in the play-offs by the Detroit Pistons.

From Player to Coach

When Wes Unseld became the coach in 1987, he joined the list of those who played for and coached the Bullets. Bob "Slick" Leonard, Kevin Loughery, Gene Shue, Unseld, and Darrell Walker make up the list, from the team's origins in Chicago through the 2010–11 season.

CHAPTER 5

FEELING THEIR WAY

The 1988–89 campaign was the start of a long funk for the Bullets. For eight straight seasons, they would have losing records and miss the playoffs. They came close to winning half their games during the first season of that stretch, going 40–42. But they finished last in the league in attendance.

From 1987 through 1991, Bernard King gave Bullets fans a consistent effort to watch. Recovering from a knee injury, he was no longer the scoring machine who had averaged nearly 33 points per game for the New York Knicks in 1984–85. But the smooth forward still scored more than 20 points per game in his first two seasons with the Bullets. Then, in 1990–91, King looked like his old self. He averaged 28.4 points per game for the Bullets. However, after the season, King

Bernard King, *right*, drives against the Jazz's Thurl Bailey in March 1988. King starred for the Bullets from 1987 to 1991, but the team struggled.

Return to Stardom

"*If I'm going to do something in life, I've always felt I had to be the best at it. That feeling drives me, gives me motivation. I knew that it would take a tremendous amount of effort to play again, but I wanted it. I didn't want to just come back, I wanted to come back as an All-Star.*"
—Forward Bernard King, on coming back from the knee injury he suffered while with the Knicks to excel with the Bullets

needed knee surgery again and missed 1991–92. The Bullets cut him loose in January 1993. He ended his career after playing that half-season for the New Jersey Nets.

From 1991 to 1995, the Bullets were among the NBA's worst teams. They lost about two-thirds of their games. They featured capable players such as forwards Harvey Grant and Pervis Ellison and guard Michael Adams. But none was an NBA star. One of the biggest changes with the team was the name change for its home arena. The Capital Centre became known as US Airways Arena in 1993.

The 1994–95 season produced a 21–61 record. But changes were happening with the roster. Early in that season, the Bullets acquired talented second-year player Chris Webber from the Golden State Warriors. Webber was selected number one overall in the 1993 NBA Draft. He joined former University of Michigan teammate Juwan Howard to give the Bullets two forwards who could score about 20 points a game.

That was also the second season for Gheorghe Muresan. Like Manute Bol, he was a 7-foot-7 center from outside the United States. However, he was not nearly as skinny as Bol. Muresan weighed about 300 pounds. Muresan,

Washington's 7-foot-7-inch center Gheorghe Muresan, *right,* defends Philadelphia's Shawn Bradley, 7 feet 6 inches, in November 1995.

from Romania, was also not as awkward as Bol on offense. Muresan did not block as many shots as Bol had. But in three of his four seasons with the Bullets, he scored at least 10 points per contest.

In 1995–96, Webber got hurt. He missed all but 15 games of the season. Still, the Bullets were a much better team, winning 39 games. The next season, things improved even more, with a return to the playoffs. The Bullets battled the Cleveland Cavaliers for the last playoff spot in the Eastern Conference. It came down to a game between the two of them in Cleveland on the last

"THE FAB FIVE"

While playing at the University of Michigan, future Bullets Chris Webber and Juwan Howard were part of a group nicknamed "the Fab Five."

The other Fab Five members were Jalen Rose, Jimmy King, and Ray Jackson. They took the University of Michigan to the National Collegiate Athletic Association tournament title game in their first two years at the school. The Wolverines lost both times, to Duke University in 1992 and to the University of North Carolina in 1993. But the Fab Five's success as freshmen and sophomores was remarkable.

Webber left Michigan after two seasons to turn professional. Rose and Howard did the same a year later. All of them were first-round selections in the NBA Draft and went on to have successful careers in the league. Howard and Webber were NBA teammates in Washington from 1994 to 1998.

day of the regular season. The Bullets won 85–81. Against Michael Jordan and the Chicago Bulls in the first round of the playoffs, the Bullets lost three straight games and were eliminated. But they played the Bulls tough. The Bullets lost the second and third games by five points and one point, respectively.

Webber and Howard combined to average 39 points per game in 1996–97. Guard Rod Strickland scored 17 per game and handed out nearly nine assists a contest.

The Bullets seemed to have reasons to be hopeful. Not only had the team played better, but it was also about to move into a new home.

The Bullets' Juwan Howard, *right*, and Chris Webber are shown in February 1997. The ex-University of Michigan teammates helped Washington reach the postseason that year.

CHAPTER **6**

MOVING DOWNTOWN

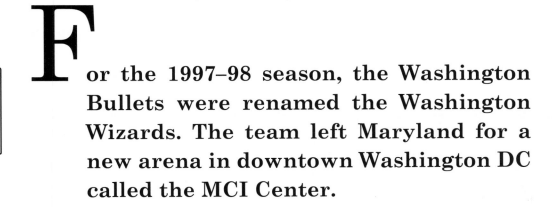

For the 1997–98 season, the Washington Bullets were renamed the Washington Wizards. The team left Maryland for a new arena in downtown Washington DC called the MCI Center.

Owner Abe Pollin decided to change the team's name because of the violence associated with the word Bullets. The Wizards had to play a few more games at the US Airways Arena in Landover, Maryland, before their new building was ready. They started playing at the MCI Center in December 1997.

Forwards Chris Webber and Juwan Howard again had strong seasons for the Wizards in 1997–98. Point guard Rod Strickland averaged more than 10 assists a game. The Wizards finished 42–40. But they lost a

Fans cheer during Washington's first game at its new home arena, the MCI Center, on December 2, 1997. Now called the Wizards, Washington beat the Seattle SuperSonics 95–78.

chance for a playoff spot on the last day of the regular season. It was the first of seven straight years for the team without a playoff berth.

Before the next season, the Wizards traded Webber to the Sacramento Kings. That deal brought All-Star guard Mitch Richmond to Washington along with a rebounding forward-center, Otis Thorpe. They did their jobs. Richmond led the Wizards in scoring. Thorpe was among the team's leaders in rebounding. But Washington had a losing record at 18–32. The season was shortened because NBA players and owners took months to reach a new labor agreement.

The biggest splash the Wizards made during this era was off the court. Michael Jordan, the legendary Chicago Bulls guard who had retired as a player in 1998, joined the Wizards in January 2000 as president of basketball operations. The Wizards could just hope that some success would rub off on them by adding Jordan.

Things did not change immediately, though the next

A Real Builder

By building an arena in downtown Washington DC with his own money, Wizards owner Abe Pollin recharged a section of the city. Most professional team owners try to get arenas and stadiums built for them with public money through deals with local or state governments. Pollin built the MCI Center with $200 million of his own money. Before the MCI Center, later to be renamed the Verizon Center, was built, there was not much business or development in that part of Washington. After the arena opened, restaurants and other businesses sprang up around the neighborhood. NBA commissioner David Stern had asked Pollin about spending so much money, $200 million, on building the arena. Pollin told him, "I don't want to be the richest man in the cemetery." Pollin died in December 2009.

Michael Jordan is shown in his first regular-season game with the Wizards on October 30, 2001. The legendary guard came out of retirement to play two seasons with Washington.

season many of the players did. In February 2001, the Wizards sent three players—including Howard—to the Dallas Mavericks in exchange for five players. But the biggest player move was to come for the 2001–02 season. Jordan decided to come out of retirement and play for the Wizards.

Jordan was 38 years old when he hit the court with Washington. Three seasons had passed since he last played for Chicago. Jordan no longer could dominate games the way he once did. Jordan played two seasons for the Wizards. He averaged 22.9 and 20 points, respectively.

Did Jordan help the Wizards? Interest in the team certainly shot up. Washington's attendance rose significantly. But Jordan did not turn the Wizards into winners. They had identical 37–45 records in 2001–02 and 2002–03.

After Jordan retired as a player again, he did not return to help run the team. The Wizards replaced him as president of basketball operations with Ernie Grunfeld. Without Jordan on the court, the Wizards won 12 fewer games in 2003–04.

In the 2001 NBA Draft, the Wizards had made a bold move. With the number one overall pick in the draft, they took Kwame Brown. He was a 6-foot-11 high school center from Brunswick, Georgia.

Brown was the first high school player ever selected with the very first pick in the draft.

The Wizards' gamble did not pay off, though. Brown lasted four seasons with Washington before the team traded him to the Los Angeles Lakers. Brown averaged at least 10 points per game just once. He never averaged more than 7.4 rebounds a game. Brown bounced around to four more teams after the Wizards.

In 2004–05, the Wizards had their first winning season in seven years and made their first playoff appearance in eight years. The Wizards had three big scoring options: guards Gilbert Arenas (25.5 points per game) and Larry Hughes (22) and forward Antawn Jamison (19.6). Washington signed Arenas as a free agent after he had played his first two NBA seasons with the Golden State

Guard Gilbert Arenas celebrates after the host Wizards beat the Bulls 94–91 in Game 6 to win a 2005 first-round playoff series. It was Washington's first postseason series victory since 1982.

Warriors. With the Wizards, he emerged as one of the league's top scorers.

In the first round of the playoffs, the Wizards faced the Bulls. With the series tied, the Wizards pulled out Game 5 on the road when Arenas made a jump shot at the buzzer. They won Game 6 at home for their first playoff series victory in 23 years. The Wizards lost in the next round to the Miami Heat. That was the first of four straight years in the playoffs for Washington.

It Did Not Pay Off

Even though he had injured his knee—which eventually required three operations—Gilbert Arenas received a huge contract from the Wizards before the 2008–09 season. He signed a six-year contract for $111 million. After he got that contract, Arenas played just 70 games for the Wizards before the team traded him in December 2010.

In 2005–06, Arenas averaged 29.3 points per game. Hughes had left as a free agent. But Jamison was still with Washington. Caron Butler joined him as another consistent scorer. The Wizards faced the Cleveland Cavaliers and their superstar, LeBron James, in the first round of the playoffs. James hit a shot with less than one second left to give Cleveland an overtime win in Game 5. The Wizards lost the next game at home and were eliminated.

Arenas continued his high-scoring ways the next season, highlighted by a 60-point game against the Los Angeles Lakers in December 2006. But by the time the Wizards reached the playoffs that year, Arenas and Butler were out with injuries. The Cavaliers swept the Wizards in the first round.

Arenas's road back from injury would be a long one. He underwent three operations on his knee and played just 13 games in 2007–08 and only two in 2008–09. The Wizards managed a winning record in 2007–08. But they fell all the way to 19–63 in 2008–09.

They only added seven more wins in 2009–10. Rookie John Wall averaged more than 15 points per game that season.

Wizards standout guard John Wall dribbles the ball up the court against the Milwaukee Bucks' John Salmons in February 2011.

TIMELINE

1961
The expansion Chicago Packers play their first NBA regular-season game on October 19, falling 120–103 to the host New York Knicks.

1962
Before the 1962–63 season, the Packers are renamed the Zephyrs.

1963
On March 25, shortly after the completion of the 1962–63 regular season, the Chicago Zephyrs move to Baltimore. The team is renamed the Bullets.

1969
The Bullets finish with a league-best 57–25 record. However, the New York Knicks sweep Baltimore in four games in the Eastern Division semifinals. The playoff appearance is the first of 12 straight for the Bullets.

1971
The Bullets finish the 1970–71 regular season barely over .500, at 42–40, but knock off the Philadelphia 76ers and the Knicks in seven-game series to reach the franchise's first NBA Finals. However, the Milwaukee Bucks sweep Baltimore in four games.

1973
The Baltimore Bullets are renamed the Capital Bullets for the 1973–74 season.

1974
The Capital Bullets are renamed the Washington Bullets before the 1974–75 season.

1975
Washington finishes the 1974–75 regular season 60–22, tied for the league's best record. The Bullets reach the NBA Finals but are swept in four games by the Golden State Warriors.

1978
The Bullets end the 1977–78 campaign with a 44–38 record, then win three playoff series to reach the NBA Finals. In Game 7 of the Finals on June 7, visiting Washington tops the Seattle SuperSonics 105–99 to capture the franchise's first NBA crown. Center-forward Wes Unseld is named Finals MVP.

1979
Washington finishes the 1978–79 regular season with the NBA's top record, 54–28. The Bullets return to the NBA Finals in a rematch against the Sonics but lose four games to one.

1988
The Bullets lose three games to two to the Detroit Pistons in the first round of the playoffs. It is the fifth straight season in which Washington falls in the first round.

1997
Washington, now nicknamed the Wizards instead of the Bullets, plays its first game at the MCI Center in Washington DC on December 2. The Wizards beat the Sonics 95–78.

2000
Legendary former Chicago Bulls guard Michael Jordan is named Wizards president of basketball operations on January 19. Jordan would then come out of retirement to play for Washington from 2001 to 2003.

2005
The Wizards, guided by guard Gilbert Arenas, finish the 2004–05 regular season 45–37 and earn the franchise's first playoff berth since 1997. Washington defeats Chicago four games to two in the first round but is swept in four games by the Miami Heat in the second round.

2010
After finishing 19–63 and 26–56 in the previous two seasons, the Wizards select guard John Wall with the first pick in the NBA Draft on June 24. Wall had been a standout at the University of Kentucky.

FRANCHISE HISTORY

Chicago Packers (1961–62)
Chicago Zephyrs (1962–63)
Baltimore Bullets (1963–73)
Capital Bullets (1973–74)
Washington Bullets (1974–97)
Washington Wizards (1997–)

NBA FINALS
(win in bold)

1971, 1975, **1978**, 1979

KEY PLAYERS
(position[s]; years with team)

Gilbert Arenas (G; 2003–2010)
Walt Bellamy (C; 1961–65)
Phil Chenier (G; 1971–79)
Bob Dandridge (F/G; 1977–81)

Elvin Hayes (F/C; 1972–81)
Antawn Jamison (F; 2004–10)
Gus Johnson (F/C; 1963–72)
Michael Jordan (G; 2001–03)
Bernard King (F; 1987–91)
Kevin Loughery (G; 1963–71)
Jeff Malone (G; 1983–90)
Earl Monroe (G; 1967–71)
Jeff Ruland (C/F; 1981–86)
Wes Unseld (C/F; 1968–81)
Chris Webber (F/C; 1994–98)

KEY COACHES

Dick Motta (1976–80):
   185–143; 27–24 (postseason)
Gene Shue (1966–73, 1980–86):
   522–505; 19–36 (postseason)

HOME ARENAS

International Amphitheater
   (1961–62)
Chicago Coliseum (1962–63)
Baltimore Civic Center (1963–73)
US Airways Arena (1973–97)
   Known as Capital Centre
   (1973–93)
Verizon Center (1997–)
   Known as MCI Center
   (1997–2006)

* All statistics through 2010–11 season

QUOTES AND ANECDOTES

"We could have lain down like puppy dogs with our stomachs in the air, but we're made of more than that." —Guard Charles Johnson, on the Bullets' 120–116 victory over the host SuperSonics in Game 4 of the 1978 NBA Finals. Washington trailed by 15 points late in the third quarter.

When the Bullets were celebrating their championship in 1978, coach Dick Motta took off his jacket and button-down shirt to reveal he was wearing a T-shirt with his often-repeated phrase, "The opera isn't over 'til the fat lady sings."

Gheorghe Muresan, a Bullet from 1993 to 1997, did not just play the role of an NBA center. He also played a giant in a movie. Muresan, who stood 7 feet 7 inches tall, appeared with actor Billy Crystal in 1998's *My Giant*.

Other names that were considered when Washington changed its nickname from the Bullets to the Wizards were Dragons, Express, Stallions, and Sea Dogs.

"He believed in people. He believed in this city when people didn't believe in this city. . . . His time here, he really made a difference." —Forward Antawn Jamison, on Wizards owner Abe Pollin

GLOSSARY

acquire

To add a player, usually through the draft, free agency, or a trade.

attendance

The number of fans at a particular game or who come to watch a team play during a particular season.

berth

A place, spot, or position, such as in the NBA playoffs.

expansion

In sports, the addition of a franchise or franchises to a league.

fast break

A style of basketball in which a team runs down the court and tries to score before the opponent's defense is set.

franchise

An entire sports organization, including the players, coaches, and staff.

intimidating

Putting fear into opponents.

outlet pass

A pass thrown by the player who gets a rebound to start a fast break.

overtime

A period in a basketball game that is played to determine a winner when the four quarters end in a tie.

pillar

In sports, a strong, reliable player whom the team is built around.

playoffs

A series of games in which the winners advance in a quest to win a championship.

trade

A move in which a player or players are sent from one team to another.

FOR MORE INFORMATION

Further Reading

Ballard, Chris. *The Art of a Beautiful Game: The Thinking Fan's Tour of the NBA.* New York: Simon & Schuster, 2009.

Shapiro, Leonard, and Andy Pollin. *The Great Book of Washington, D.C. Sports Lists.* Philadelphia: Running Press, 2008.

Simmons, Bill. *The Book of Basketball: The NBA According to the Sports Guy.* New York: Random House, 2009.

Web Links

To learn more about the Washington Wizards, visit ABDO Publishing Company online at **www.abdopublishing.com**. Web sites about the Wizards are featured on our Book Links page. These links are routinely monitored and updated to provide the most current information available.

Places to Visit

1st Mariner Arena
201 West Baltimore Street
Baltimore, MD 21201
410-347-2020
www.baltimorearena.com
This is the former home of the Baltimore Bullets. It was called the Baltimore Civic Center when they played there from 1963 to 1973.

Naismith Memorial Basketball Hall of Fame
1000 West Columbus Avenue
Springfield, MA 01105
413-781-6500
www.hoophall.com
This hall of fame and museum highlights the greatest players and moments in basketball history. Elvin Hayes and Wes Unseld are among the ex-players from the Wizards franchise enshrined here.

Verizon Center
601 F Street, Northwest
Washington, DC 20004
202-661-5000
www.verizoncenter.com
This has been the Wizards' home arena since 1997, when it was known as the MCI Center. The venue's name was changed in 2006.

INDEX

About the Author

Ray Frager is a freelance writer based in the Baltimore, Maryland, area. He has been a professional sports editor and writer since 1980. He has worked for the *Trenton Times*, the *Dallas Morning News*, the *Baltimore Sun*, and FOXSports.com. At the *Sun*, he edited books on Cal Ripken Jr., the building of Baltimore's football stadium, and the Baltimore Ravens' 2000 Super Bowl season. He has written books on the Baltimore Orioles and the Pittsburgh Pirates.